Simon Hopkinson

Liver, Sweetbreads and Kidneys

SIMON HOPKINSON

Liver, Sweetbreads and Kidneys

Photography by Philip Wilkins

WEIDENFELD & NICOLSON

Simon Hopkinson

Simon Hopkinson grew up in Bury, Lancashire, where his love of eating was established at the kitchen table. At seventeen, he left school to join the kitchens of Yves Champeau at the Normandie in Birtle, a restaurant highly acclaimed in the 1960s and 1970s and where the regional French cooking made a lasting impression on him. There followed a succession of jobs, culminating in the Shed restaurant at Dinas, near Fishguard, Pembrokeshire, where he set himself up on his own, one month before his 21st birthday.

Three years later, itchy to come to London, he landed a job with the Egon Ronay Organisation as an inspector, which he enjoyed doing for just over two years. Then, keen to cook again, he took a post as chef in a private house in Chelsea. He stayed there for three years, returning to the restaurant scene in 1983 as chef at Hilaire in London's Old Brompton Road.

While at Hilaire, a friendship developed with one particular customer, Terence Conran, which led to the opening of Bibendum, in the restored Michelin Building in nearby Fulham Road, in 1987. A partnership followed with Terence Conran and Paul Hamlyn, the publisher, which remains to this day, although Simon retired from 'flinging a few pans around' in January 1995 to concentrate more on writing.

This had begun with the award-winning *Roast Chicken and Other Stories* (both André Simon Memorial and Glenfiddich Food Book of the Year in 1995) which he wrote with the help of Lindsey Bareham. Since then, he has had a monthly column in *Sainsbury's The Magazine* since its inception in May 1994 and he writes for *The Independent* newspaper every week. He has also contributed a sizeable chunk of recipes to the new *Conran Cookbook* and has written another book in collaboration with Lindsey Bareham, entitled *The Prawn Cocktail Years*; both books will be published in 1997.

Contents

The basics

Kissing don't last,
cookery do.

GEORGE MEREDITH, 1828–1909

Introduction

Cooking offal of any kind has always appealed to me. There is something so endlessly seductive about the textures, whether it be the melting tenderness of a veal sweetbread, the tender yet attractively bouncy feel of grilled veal kidney or the soft richness of a thick slice of calves' liver. Their flavours, too, are deep and intriguing, with liver, perhaps, being the most widely appreciated, particularly when it is from a duck or goose, having been fattened on corn for most of its short life. The liver from a calf is equally superb, and when cooked by Italians – who know better than anyone else how to cook it – the results can be truly wonderful.

Kidneys, on the other hand, have a more assertive appeal. The smell of them cooking is immediately obvious, particularly when given brisk treatment such as grilling. Only lambs' and calves' kidneys can stand a searing heat; beef kidneys are good when braised or put into a pudding, while pigs' kidneys need more careful treatment, though if you happen to find some attached to a pork chop (a rare treat these days) don't cut it off, as it is the best bit.

Sweetbreads are something else altogether. Their texture is so soft and creamy you wonder how the simple workings of an animal could produce such a luxurious organ. They carry a luxurious price tag too, particularly those from a calf (known in French, and in many recipes, as *ris de veau*), although the sweetbreads from the first spring lambs are not exactly to be had for ready money. Recipes are given for both, but they are interchangeable.

Simon Hopkinson

BREADCRUMBED VEAL SWEETBREADS
with sauce gribiche

SERVES 4

600 – 800 g/1¼ – 1¾ lb veal
   sweetbreads, part-cooked
   and peeled (page 35)
1 tablespoon plain flour
1 large egg, beaten
3 – 4 tablespoons fresh white
   breadcrumbs
2 tablespoons olive oil
50 g/2 oz butter

Sauce gribiche

1 tablespoon smooth
   Dijon mustard
2 tablespoons tarragon vinegar
salt and pepper
275 – 325 ml/9 – 11 fl oz
   groundnut or sunflower oil
1½ tablespoons capers,
   drained, squeezed dry
   and coarsely chopped
5 sprigs of tarragon, leaves only,
   finely chopped
5 hard-boiled eggs, yolks only,
   sieved

To serve

1 lemon, cut into quarters
sprigs of watercress or tarragon

To make the sauce, blend the mustard, vinegar, salt and pepper in a liquidizer or whisk together in a bowl. With the motor running (or still whisking), start pouring in the oil in a thin stream. When you have added about three-quarters of the oil, switch off and taste for acidity and seasoning. Continue adding more oil if necessary. The finished sauce should have the consistency of thick, just pourable, double cream; it may need thinning down with a little lukewarm water. When the basic dressing is complete, stir in the capers, tarragon and egg yolks.

Cut the prepared sweetbreads into approximately twelve pieces. Put the flour, beaten egg and bread-crumbs in three saucers. Coat each piece of sweetbread in the flour, then the egg and finally the breadcrumbs.

Heat the oil and butter together in a large frying pan, until foaming. Gently lay in the sweetbreads and cook over a low heat for about 4–5 minutes on each side, until crusted and golden. Remove with a slotted spoon and drain on paper towels.

Put the sweetbreads into a warmed serving dish and garnish with lemon wedges and watercress or tarragon. Hand the sauce separately.

Excellent served with chips and perhaps a fiery rocket salad. As an alternative to sauce gribiche, make a rich béarnaise (page 37). Follow with apple or pear tart and whipped cream.

SMOOTH CHICKEN LIVER PÂTÉ
with Armagnac and sultanas

SERVES 4

40 g/1½ oz sultanas

3 tablespoons port

2 tablespoons Armagnac

350 g/13 oz chicken livers, trimmed (page 34)

100 g/3½ oz unsalted butter, softened

85 ml/3 fl oz double cream, warmed

¼ teaspoon ground allspice

1 teaspoon salt

½ teaspoon pepper

50 g/2 oz butter, melted

Put the sultanas in a small bowl, warm the port and Armagnac together and pour over the sultanas. Leave to soak for 30 minutes.

Meanwhile, poach the livers in simmering salted water for a couple of minutes, until just bouncy and tight but not firm (lift one out with a slotted spoon to test); overcooking will result in grey pâté. Drain and tip into a food processor or liquidizer. Add the sultana soaking liquid, the softened butter, cream, allspice, salt and pepper and blend briefly, until smooth. Fold in the sultanas, then pour into a shallow dish and smooth the surface with a spatula. Cover with cling film and put into the refrigerator to chill for 30 minutes.

Remove the cling film and carefully spoon over the melted butter to seal. Return to the refrigerator for at least 6 hours or overnight. Eat within 48 hours, with hot toast.

Follow this rich first course with either a simple roast chicken cooked with tarragon or a handsome piece of baked cod with olive oil and fresh herbs. Serve with green beans and new potatoes.

BROCHETTE OF LAMBS' KIDNEYS
with pancetta, thyme and polenta

SERVES 4

10 lambs' kidneys, skinned and
   cored (page 34), then cut into
   four equal chunks
7–8 thickish slices of rindless
   pancetta or streaky bacon,
   cut into 32 small squares
12–15 small sprigs of thyme
4–5 tablespoons olive oil
3–4 garlic cloves, bruised
sea salt and black pepper

Polenta
1.2 litres/2 pints water
1½ teaspoons salt
200 g/7 oz coarse polenta
50–85 g/2–3 oz butter,
   cut into cubes
freshly ground white pepper
40 g/1½ oz Parmesan cheese,
   grated

Soak 8 wooden skewers in warm water for 20 minutes.

Thread 5 kidney pieces on to each skewer, alternating
with pieces of bacon and adding the sprigs of thyme
intermittently. Put the skewers in a shallow dish, pour
over the olive oil, tuck in the garlic cloves and grind over
plenty of pepper – do not add salt at this stage. Leave to
marinate for 45 minutes while you prepare the polenta.

Bring the water and salt to the boil in a large, heavy-
bottomed saucepan. Start to stir the water with a balloon
whisk. With your other hand, trickle the polenta into
the water in a steady, fine, sand-like stream. Do not stop
whisking until all the polenta has been added. Lower the
heat and continue whisking for a few moments, then
turn the heat as low as possible and start to stir with a
wooden spoon. Continue stirring over a very low heat
for about 30–40 minutes; the polenta is ready when it
starts to come away from the sides of the pan. Stir in the
butter piece by piece, add the pepper and Parmesan, and
keep warm in the pan.

Heat a ribbed stove-top grill pan until it is hot, but not
red hot. Lift the skewers from the oil, shaking off any
excess, and place on the hot grill. Cook for about 10–12
minutes, depending on how pink you like your kidneys,
turning from time to time until browned on all sides.

Pile the polenta on to four warmed plates and place two
brochettes on top. Sprinkle with sea salt and serve at once.

*A salad of crisp chicory with a perky mustard vinaigrette would
go down very well. As this is a fairly hefty dish, serve a light
pudding such as a fresh fruit jelly or fruit salad.*

Calves' liver Venetian style

SERVES 4

3 tablespoons light olive oil

3 mild Spanish onions, very
thinly sliced

salt and pepper

40 g/1½ oz butter

8 very thin slices of calves' liver,
cut into small squares

1 tablespoon chopped fresh
parsley

1–2 tablespoons red wine
vinegar

Heat the olive oil in a frying pan, add the onions and
cook over a low heat until meltingly tender and soft.
It doesn't matter if they take on a little colour, but the
most important thing is that they cook slowly – which
can take up to 30 minutes. Season with salt and pepper.

The final assembly of the dish should not take more
than about 1 minute. Heat the butter in a large frying
pan until foaming. Season the liver with salt and pepper
and toss in the butter for about 20 seconds. Transfer
to a colander. Put the onions into the pan and toss
briefly until golden brown. Return the liver to the
pan together with the parsley, and stir in the vinegar.
Serve at once, on warmed plates.

*This dish is good served with wet polenta (page 14), or
perhaps some buttery mashed potatoes. A green salad dressed
with lemon juice and good olive oil, and eaten with ripe
gorgonzola cheese, would be a fitting follow-up.*

BLANQUETTE OF SWEETBREADS
with cream and lemon

SERVES 4

40 g/1½ oz butter
2 shallots, finely chopped
100 ml/3½ fl oz dry white wine
3 strips of thinly pared
    lemon rind
3 sprigs of thyme
100 ml/3½ fl oz chicken stock
675 g/1½ lb lambs'
    sweetbreads, blanched and
    peeled (page 35)
2 egg yolks
150 ml/5 fl oz double cream
juice of 1 small lemon
1 tablespoon chopped
    fresh parsley

Melt the butter in a saucepan, add the shallots and cook over a low heat until soft but not browned. Add the wine, lemon rind and thyme and simmer for 5 minutes. Add the stock and bring back to the boil. Simmer over a low heat until reduced by half.

Add the prepared sweetbreads to the pan and simmer for 15−20 minutes, until they are firm, but give a little when squeezed (lift one out with a slotted spoon to test). When the sweetbreads are ready, transfer them to an ovenproof dish, shaking off any bits of shallot, cover the dish and keep warm in a low oven.

Strain the cooking liquid into a clean saucepan and bring back to a simmer. Beat together the egg yolks and cream and pour into the pan, whisking constantly until well blended. Cook over a very low heat until thickened: do not boil. Stir in the lemon juice and parsley and return the sweetbreads to the sauce to heat through. Turn into a warmed dish and serve at once.

A rich and creamy dish such as this cries out for a simple vegetable such as fresh peas or broad beans. A few sautéed button mushrooms might be another option. Follow with the first strawberries of the season, simply dressed with a little sugar and lemon juice.

GRILLED CALVES' LIVER
with guacamole

SERVES 4

4 slices of calves' liver,
  total weight 350 – 400 g/
  13 –14 oz
salt and pepper
olive oil

Guacamole

2 ripe Hass avocados,
  coarsely chopped
juice of 1 lime
2 large green chillies,
  not too fiery, seeded
  and finely chopped
8 mint leaves, finely chopped
1 tablespoon finely chopped
  fresh coriander
2 tablespoons virgin olive oil
2 spring onions, finely chopped
2 ripe tomatoes, skinned,
  seeded and finely chopped
1 garlic clove, crushed to a paste
  with a little salt

To serve

sprigs of fresh coriander
a little extra virgin olive oil
4 lime wedges

First make the guacamole. Mix all the ingredients in a bowl, press a piece of cling film over the surface and set aside.

Heat a ribbed stove-top grill pan (not a radiant grill, as this results in a steaming slice of hot liver) until very hot. Season the liver, brush with olive oil and place on the hot grill. Cook for about 1 minute on each side, so the surfaces are nicely striped from the grill.

Serve at once on four warmed plates and pile some of the guacamole alongside each serving. Garnish with coriander sprigs, sprinkle a little extra virgin olive oil over the liver and put a lime wedge on each plate.

Chips or fried potatoes with onions sounds good here – and maybe a crisp green salad dressed with olive oil and Parmesan cheese – even a Caesar salad, although that might be more fitting as a first course. How about a slice of lemon tart to finish with?

CALVES' LIVER STEAK
with Cumberland sauce

SERVES 4

2 thick slices of calves' liver,
  about 350 g/13 oz each,
  cut in half
salt and pepper
olive oil

Cumberland sauce

2 oranges
2 lemons
1 small jar (about 175 g/6 oz)
  redcurrant jelly
150 ml/5 fl oz port
1 large piece of fresh
  ginger, grated
2 teaspoons English
  mustard powder
1 teaspoon arrowroot

First make the sauce. Thinly pare the rind of the oranges and lemons and cut into very thin strips. Blanch in a small saucepan of boiling water for 20 seconds, then drain and rinse under cold running water. Dry on paper towels and reserve. Squeeze the juice from the oranges and lemons and put into a stainless steel or other non-reactive saucepan. Add the jelly, port and ginger, bring to a simmer and cook for 10 minutes. Strain through a fine sieve and then pour back into the cleaned pan. Mix the mustard and arrowroot together with 2 tablespoons water until smooth. Add to the port/jelly liquid and whisk together. Bring back to a simmer and cook for a few minutes until shiny and thickened. Stir in the reserved orange and lemon rind and keep warm.

Heat a ribbed stove-top grill pan (not a radiant grill, as this results in a steaming slice of hot liver) until hot, but not red hot. Season the liver, brush with olive oil and place on the hot grill. Cook for about 1 minute, then turn through 45 degrees to give the meat the traditional criss-cross pattern; cook for 1 minute more. Repeat on the other side. If the liver is particularly thick, it will need slightly longer cooking times; the texture, when prodded with your finger, should still be bouncy. Place in a very low oven for a minute or two, so that the meat has a chance to rest. Slice the liver and spoon over the sauce.

Serve with a potato dish such as pommes boulangère (sliced potatoes and onions baked in stock) and perhaps a dish of buttered spinach. Follow with an English pudding, but something not too sweet, such as a milky rice pudding.

BUTTERED VEAL SWEETBREADS
with asparagus and morels

SERVES 4

600–800 g/1¼–1¾ lb veal
   sweetbreads, part-cooked
   and peeled (page 35)
250 g/9 oz fresh asparagus
salt and pepper
50 g/2 oz butter
125 g/4 oz fresh morel
   mushrooms (or about 25 g/
   1 oz dried morels, soaked
   in a little warm water for
   20 minutes)
1 tablespoon snipped
   fresh chives

Butter sauce
juice of 1 large lemon
100 g/3½ oz butter, cut into
   small chunks

Cut the prepared sweetbreads into generous chunks. Trim the asparagus and peel the ends of any tough parts. Cut into small lengths, on the diagonal. Bring a large saucepan of water to the boil, add a good pinch of salt and when the water is boiling vigorously add the asparagus. Boil rapidly for about 2 minutes, until the asparagus is just tender. Drain, refresh under cold running water, drain well and set aside.

Melt half the butter in a large frying pan, add the morels, season and cook for a few minutes until softened. Stir in the asparagus and heat through. Tip into a warmed serving dish, cover and keep warm in a low oven.

Add the remaining butter to the pan and heat until foaming. Season the sweetbreads and fry briskly until pale golden. Remove from the heat, cover the pan and keep warm while you make the butter sauce.

Put the lemon juice in a small saucepan with 2 table-spoons water and heat gently until slightly syrupy and reduced by about two-thirds. Turn the heat as low as possible and whisk in the butter, bit by bit, until you have a creamy-textured sauce. Season, and add a final squeeze of lemon juice. Keep warm.

To serve, tip the cooked asparagus and morels back into the frying pan with the sweetbreads, mix carefully and then add the butter sauce. Warm through, spoon back into the serving dish and sprinkle with the chives.

This is a dish for late spring, when fresh morels and asparagus are in season. I might consider the first Jersey Royal new potatoes an essential accompaniment. Some simple stewed rhubarb or a fool would make an ideal pudding.

VEAL KIDNEYS
with bone marrow and persillade

SERVES 4

4 beef marrow bones, sawn into
    5 cm/2 inch pieces*
100 g/3½ oz fresh breadcrumbs
1 large bunch of flat-leaf parsley,
    leaves only, coarsely chopped
3 garlic cloves, chopped
thinly pared rind of 1 large
    lemon, chopped
2 small veal kidneys, trimmed
    and cored (page 34), then
    sliced 1 cm/½ inch thick
salt and pepper
olive oil

To serve
4 lemon wedges

* Ask the butcher to saw the
marrow bones.

Soak the marrow bones in cold water for 30 minutes to rid them of excess blood. To remove the marrow, simply push it through the bone with your fingers. Slice into thin circles and keep in a cool place.

To make the persillade, put the breadcrumbs into a food processor with the parsley, garlic and lemon rind. Process until well blended, but don't overwork the crumbs; they should not become paste-like.

Heat a ribbed stove-top grill pan until very hot; also heat a radiant grill. Season the kidneys and brush with a little olive oil on each side. Place on the hot grill pan and cook for 1–2 minutes on each side – you may have to do this in two batches.

Place the kidneys on a baking sheet and lay 2–3 slices of the bone marrow on each slice. Sprinkle carefully with the persillade crumbs and trickle a tiny amount of olive oil over each. Place under the grill and cook until the crumbs are slightly browned and the marrow underneath has softened. Serve immediately with the lemon wedges.

This is a fairly rich dish, so perhaps a small bowl of boiled runner beans or purple sprouting broccoli would be appropriate. Follow with some poached fruits such as plums or apricots, served with cold thin custard sauce.

Steak, kidney and potato pie

SERVES 4

300 g/11 oz stewing steak,
   cut into 1 cm/½ inch dice
150 g/5 oz ox kidney, cut into
   1 cm/½ inch pieces
200 g/7 oz onion, chopped
200 g/7 oz peeled potato, diced
2 teaspoons plain flour
salt and pepper
300 g/11 oz pie pastry
   (page 36)
1 small egg, beaten

Preheat the oven to 200°C/400°F/Gas Mark 6 and put a baking sheet on the middle shelf to heat up, so that the base of the pie will cook through. Lightly butter a 20 cm/8 inch diameter loose-bottomed tin, 4 cm/1½ inches deep.

Put the steak, kidney, onion, potato, flour, salt and pepper into a large bowl and mix together with your hands.

Cut off about two-thirds of the pastry and roll out on a lightly floured surface to form a circle about 3 mm/⅛ inch thick – not too thin. Line the tin with the pastry, leaving it overhanging at the edges. Roll out the rest of the pastry for the lid and set aside. Pile the filling into the tin and carefully pour in 125 ml/4 fl oz cold water, which should just reach the surface. Brush the overhanging edge of the pastry with water and put the pastry lid on top. Press the edges together and then slice off the excess pastry with a knife.

Brush the pastry with beaten egg, then decorate with pastry trimmings and crimp the edges together with a fork. Make two incisions in the centre of the pie and place in the oven. Cook for 25 minutes, and then turn the temperature down to 160°C/325°F/Gas Mark 3. Bake for a further 1½ hours, checking from time to time that the pastry is not browning too much; if it is, then turn the oven down further. Remove from the oven and leave to rest for 10 minutes before serving.

There really isn't any room for anything else here, except something sharp such as pickled red cabbage or piccalilli; I might also reach for the ketchup bottle.

A SMALL STEW OF VEAL OFFAL,
with Madeira and a pig's trotter

SERVES 4

25 g/1 oz butter
1 onion, chopped
2 sticks of celery, chopped
1 carrot, chopped
2 garlic cloves, bruised
2 teaspoons tomato purée
2 teaspoons plain flour
150 ml/5 fl oz dry white wine
150 ml/5 fl oz Madeira, plus
    2 tablespoons
250 ml/8 fl oz well–flavoured
    beef or veal stock
2 teaspoons redcurrant jelly
bouquet garni
1 pig's trotter (page 34)
3–4 tablespoons olive oil
250 g/9 oz veal sweetbreads,
    part-cooked and peeled
    (page 35)
250 g/9 oz veal kidney, cut into
    2 cm/¾ inch lobes
250 g/9 oz calves' liver, in a
    thick piece, cut into 2 cm/
    ¾ inch chunks
salt and pepper
12 small carrots, boiled
12 button onions, glazed
    (page 36)
12 tiny new potatoes, boiled
1 tablespoon chopped
    fresh tarragon

Preheat the oven to 140°C/275°F/Gas Mark 1.

In a heavy-bottomed casserole, melt the butter, add the onion, celery and carrot and fry until well browned. Add the garlic and tomato purée and cook until rust coloured. Add the flour and stir over the heat for 2 minutes. Pour in the wine and 150 ml/5 fl oz Madeira and stir well. Bring to a simmer and cook until reduced by one-third. Add the stock, redcurrant jelly and bouquet garni. Bring back to a simmer and immerse the prepared trotter. Cover with a lid and place in the oven for about 1½ hours.

Meanwhile, heat 1 tablespoon of the olive oil in a frying pan until smoking. Cut the sweetbreads into chunks and fry until golden brown. Transfer to a plate and set aside to cool. Using the remaining oil, sear the kidney and liver in the same way.

Remove the casserole from the oven and tip into a colander set over a bowl. Leave for a few minutes, then remove the trotter, pick all the meat from the bones and chop into small pieces. Set aside with the other meats.

Strain the trotter liquid through a fine sieve, back into the (cleaned) casserole and leave to settle for a few minutes. Skim a few paper towels over the surface to remove any fat. Taste and adjust the seasoning. Bring the sauce to a simmer and add the seared meats, the carrots, button onions, potatoes, tarragon and extra Madeira. Bring back to a simmer and simmer gently for 7–10 minutes. Serve hot.

This stew cries out for a vegetable purée, such as parsnips, swede or celeriac, to soak up the delicious gravy. Follow with a traditional fruit crumble.

GRILLED CALVES' KIDNEYS
with coriander, lime and chilli butter

SERVES 4

2 small veal kidneys, trimmed
    and cored (page 34), then
    sliced 1 cm/½ inch thick
salt and pepper
olive oil

Coriander, lime and chilli butter

125 g/4 oz butter, softened
3 tablespoons virgin olive oil
2 teaspoons Asian fish sauce
    (optional)
2 large red chillies, not too fiery,
    seeded and finely chopped
2 tablespoons chopped fresh
    coriander
grated zest of 1 lime
juice of 2 limes

To serve

sprigs of coriander
a little extra virgin olive oil

First make the coriander, lime and chilli butter. Place all the ingredients in a food processor, add a little salt and blend thoroughly (use the plastic mixing blade rather than the sharp metal one). Wrap in a sheet of dampened greaseproof paper and form a sausage shape by squeezing the ends together like a Christmas cracker. Place in the refrigerator for at least 30 minutes to firm up.

Heat a ribbed stove-top grill pan until very hot. Season the kidneys and brush with a little olive oil on each side. Place on the hot grill pan and cook for 1–2 minutes on each side – you may have to do this in two batches.

Serve the kidneys on four warmed plates. Unwrap the butter, cut into thin slices and place a slice on each piece of kidney. Garnish with sprigs of coriander and sprinkle with a little extra virgin olive oil. The residual heat of the kidneys will partly melt the butter as it goes to table.

The spicy flavours in this dish suggest the accompaniment of stir-fried vegetables: a single variety or perhaps a mixture. Onions, peppers, aubergines and courgettes, spiced with cumin and coriander, might be seen as Asian ratatouille, but would be delicious. Fresh lychees, peeled and eaten at table, would be a fitting conclusion.

The Basics

BUYING AND PREPARING OFFAL

You should be able to buy fresh offal from good butchers, but be prepared to order it a few days ahead. I would never recommend using frozen offal.

LIVER

Use a sharp knife to trim off any veins, then gently peel off and discard the surface membrane. Chicken and duck livers should be inspected for any green-tinged areas, which must be trimmed off.

KIDNEYS

Peel off and discard the surface membrane. Cut the kidney in half lengthways and cut out as much of the core as you wish, using a small sharp knife or scissors.

PIGS' TROTTERS

Trotters are sometimes blanched before use: to do this, put them in a saucepan with cold water to cover, bring to the boil, then simmer for 2–3 minutes. Drain and rinse in cold water. However, they will have been treated by the butcher, so this is not really necessary.

For the stew on page 30, ask the butcher to split a trotter in half. When you get it home, singe off any hairs, using a blowtorch or over a gas flame.

SWEETBREADS

TO BLANCH

500 g–1 kg/1–2 lb veal
  sweetbreads (according
  to recipe)
juice of 1 lemon
salt

Trim off any unsightly bits and pieces from the sweet-breads and rinse under cold running water for a few minutes. Drain, then put into a stainless steel or other non-reactive saucepan. Just cover with cold water and add the lemon juice and a little salt. Bring to a simmer, cook for 1 minute, then drain in a colander.

Refresh under cold water, then lay out on a plate or chopping board. Pick over each piece and peel off the thin membrane using a small, sharp knife.

TO PART-COOK

500 g–1 kg/1–2 lb veal
  sweetbreads (according
  to recipe)
juice of 1 lemon
1 onion, sliced
1 large carrot, sliced
2 sprigs of thyme
2 bay leaves
salt
a few peppercorns

Trim off any unsightly bits and pieces from the sweet-breads and rinse under cold running water for a few minutes. Drain, then put into a stainless steel or other non-reactive saucepan. Just cover with cold water and add the lemon juice, onion, carrot, herbs, a little salt and the peppercorns. Bring to a simmer, then simmer very gently for about 7–10 minutes.

Drain in a colander and refresh under cold water, then lay out on a plate or chopping board. Pick over each piece and peel off the thin membrane using a small, sharp knife.

PIE PASTRY

Makes 300 g/11 oz

150 g/5 oz dripping or lard, very
    cold from the refrigerator and
    cut into small pieces
300 g/11 oz plain flour, sifted
salt
4–5 tablespoons iced water

Rub together the fat, flour and salt until it resembles coarse breadcrumbs. Quickly mix in the water, until the mixture comes together. Knead lightly and put into a plastic bag. Leave to rest in the refrigerator for 30 minutes.

GLAZED ONIONS

Serves 4 as an accompaniment

12–20 button onions
25–50 g/1–2 oz butter

Pop the onions into a saucepan of boiling water for 1 minute, then drain, refresh under cold water, and peel.

Melt the butter in a saucepan just large enough to hold the onions in a single layer. Add the onions and cook over a low heat until glazed and tender.

Béarnaise sauce

Makes 250 ml/8 fl oz

3 tablespoons white
    wine vinegar

3 tablespoons dry white wine

1 shallot, finely chopped

10 peppercorns

2 tablespoons chopped
    fresh tarragon

2 egg yolks

125 g/4 oz butter, cut into
    small pieces

½ lemon

salt and cayenne pepper

Put the vinegar, wine, shallot, peppercorns and half the tarragon into a small saucepan (not aluminium), bring to the boil, then boil until reduced to 2 tablespoons. Leave to cool.

Bring a large saucepan of water to the boil. Beat the egg yolks with 1 tablespoon water, then whisk them into the reduced liquid. Whisking constantly, lower the small saucepan into the pan of boiling water and whisk until the yolks begin to thicken. Whisk in the butter, piece by piece, to make a thick sauce. Strain the sauce, stir in the remaining tarragon, then taste and adjust the seasoning with lemon juice, salt and cayenne pepper. Serve warm.

Classic Cooking

STARTERS
Lesley Waters A former chef and now a popular television cook, appearing regularly on *Ready Steady Cook* and *Can't Cook Won't Cook*. Author of several cookery books.

VEGETABLE SOUPS
Elisabeth Luard Cookery writer for the *Sunday Telegraph Magazine* and author of *European Peasant Food* and *European Festival Food*, which won a Glenfiddich Award.

GOURMET SALADS
Sonia Stevenson The first woman chef in the UK to be awarded a Michelin star, at the Horn of Plenty in Devon. Author of *The Magic of Saucery* and *Fresh Ways with Fish*.

FISH AND SHELLFISH
Gordon Ramsay Chef/proprietor of London's Aubergine restaurant, recently awarded its second Michelin star, and author of *A Passion for Flavour*.

CHICKEN, DUCK AND GAME
Nick Nairn Chef/patron of Braeval restaurant near Aberfoyle in Scotland, whose BBC-TV series *Wild Harvest* was last summer's most successful cookery series, accompanied by a book.

LIVERS, SWEETBREADS AND KIDNEYS
Simon Hopkinson Former chef/patron at London's Bibendum restaurant, columnist and author of *Roast Chicken and Other Stories* and *The Prawn Cocktail Years*.

VEGETARIAN
Rosamond Richardson Author of several vegetarian titles, including *The Great Green Cookbook* and *Food from Green Places*.

PASTA
Joy Davies One of the creators of *BBC Good Food Magazine*, she has been food editor of *She, Woman* and *Options* and written for the *Guardian, Daily Telegraph* and *Harpers & Queen*.

CHEESE DISHES
Rose Elliot The UK's most successful vegetarian cookery writer and author of many books, including *Not Just a Load of Old Lentils* and *The Classic Vegetarian Cookbook*.

POTATO DISHES
Patrick McDonald Former chef/patron of the acclaimed Epicurean restaurant in Cheltenham, and food consultant to Sir Rocco Forte Hotels.

BISTRO
Anne Willan Founder and director of La Varenne Cookery School in Burgundy and West Virginia. Author of many books and a specialist in French cuisine.

ITALIAN
Anna Del Conte Author of several books on Italian food, including *The Gastronomy of Italy, Secrets from an Italian Kitchen* and *The Classic Food of Northern Italy* (chosen as the 1996 Guild of Food Writers Book of the Year).

Vietnamese
Nicole Routhier One of the United States' most popular cookery writers, her books include *Cooking Under Wraps, Nicole Routhier's Fruit Cookbook* and the award-winning *The Foods of Vietnam*.

Malaysian
Jill Dupleix One of Australia's best known cookery writers and broadcasters, with columns in the *Sydney Morning Herald* and *Elle*. Her books include *New Food* and *Allegro al dente*.

Peking Cuisine
Helen Chen Author of *Chinese Home Cooking*, she learned to cook traditional Peking dishes from her mother, Joyce Chen, the *grande dame* of Chinese cooking in the United States.

Stir-fries
Kay Fairfax A writer and broadcaster whose books include *100 Great Stir-fries, Homemade* and *The Australian Christmas Book*.

Noodles
Terry Durack Australia's most widely read restaurant critic and co-editor of the *Sydney Morning Herald Good Food Guide*. He is the author of *YUM*, a book of stories and recipes.

North Indian Curries
Pat Chapman Founded the Curry Club in 1982. A regular broadcaster on television and radio, he is the author of 20 books, which have sold more than 1 million copies.

Grills and Barbecues
Brian Turner Chef/patron of Turner's in Knightsbridge and one of Britain's most popular food broadcasters; he appears frequently on *Ready Steady Cook, Food and Drink* and many other television programmes.

Summer and Winter Casseroles
Anton Edelmann Maître Chef des Cuisines at the Savoy Hotel, London. Author of six cookery books, he has also appeared on television.

Traditional Puddings
Tessa Bramley Chef/patron of the acclaimed Old Vicarage restaurant in Ridgeway, Derbyshire and author of *The Instinctive Cook*.

Decorated Cakes
Jane Asher Author of several cookery books and a novel. She has also appeared in her own television series, *Jane Asher's Christmas* (1995).

Favourite Cakes
Mary Berry One of Britain's leading cookery writers, her numerous books include *Mary Berry's Ultimate Cake Book*. She has made many television and radio appearances.

Ice Creams and Semi Freddi
Ann and Franco Taruschio Owners of the renowned Walnut Tree Inn near Abergavenny in Wales, soon to appear in a television series, *Franco and Friends: Food from the Walnut Tree*. They have written three books together.

First published in 1997 by
George Weidenfeld & Nicolson
The Orion Publishing Group
Orion House
5 Upper St Martin's Lane
London WC2H 9EA

British Library Cataloguing-in-Publication data
A catalogue record for this book is available from
the British Library

ISBN 0 297 82275 6

Designed by Lucy Holmes
Edited by Maggie Ramsay
Food styling by Louise Pickford
Typesetting by Tiger Typeset

The Calamity of the Prophet's Death, and its Effects on the Muslim Nation

Authored by
Ḥusayn al-ʿAwāyishah

Translated by
Faisal Ibn Muhammad

ISBN 1 898649 58 8

British Library Cataloguing in Publication Data.

A catalogue record for this book is available from the British Library.

Published: Al-Hidaayah Publishing and Distribution

Distributed by: Al-Hidaayah Publishing and Distribution

                      P.O. Box 3332

                      Birmingham

                      United Kingdom

                      B10 0UH

                      Tel: 0121 753 1889

                      Fax: 0121 753 2422

                      Website: www.al-hidaayah.co.uk

                      Email: mail@al-hidaayah.co.uk

Contents

Transliteration Table

Consonants,

ء	ʾ	د	d	ض	ḍ	ك	k
ب	b	ذ	dh	ط	ṭ	ل	l
ت	t	ر	r	ظ	ẓ	م	m
ث	th	ز	z	ع	ʿ	ن	n
ج	j	س	s	غ	gh	ه	h
ح	ḥ	ش	sh	ف	f	و	w
خ	kh	ص	ṣ	ق	q	ي	y

Vowels, diphthongs, etc.

Short:		‒َ	a	‒ِ	i	‒ُ	u
Long:		‒ َا	ā	‒ِي	ī	‒ُو	ū
diphthongs:				‒َى	ay	‒َو	aw

The Calamity of the Prophet's Death, and its
Effects on the Muslim Nation

Introduction

Indeed, all praise is for Allāh; we praise Him, repent to Him, and seek His forgiveness and help. We seek refuge in Allāh from the evil of our own selves and of our wicked deeds. Whomsoever Allāh guides, none can lead astray; and whomsoever Allāh leads astray, none can guide. And I bear witness that none has the right to be worshipped except Allāh alone, and He has no partner; and I bear witness that our Prophet Muḥammad is His slave and Messenger.

يَٰٓأَيُّهَا ٱلَّذِينَ ءَامَنُوا۟ ٱتَّقُوا۟ ٱللَّهَ حَقَّ تُقَاتِهِۦ وَلَا تَمُوتُنَّ إِلَّا وَأَنتُم مُّسْلِمُونَ ۝

O you who believe! Fear Allāh (ﷻ) (by doing all that He has ordered and by abstaining from all that He has forbidden) as He should be feared. [Obey Him, be thankful to Him, and remember Him always], and die not except in the state of Islām (as Muslims) with complete submission to Allāh (ﷻ). (Qur'ān 3:102)

يَٰٓأَيُّهَا ٱلنَّاسُ ٱتَّقُوا۟ رَبَّكُمُ ٱلَّذِى خَلَقَكُم مِّن نَّفْسٍ وَٰحِدَةٍ وَخَلَقَ مِنْهَا زَوْجَهَا وَبَثَّ مِنْهُمَا رِجَالًا كَثِيرًا وَنِسَآءً وَٱتَّقُوا۟ ٱللَّهَ ٱلَّذِى تَسَآءَلُونَ بِهِۦ وَٱلْأَرْحَامَ إِنَّ ٱللَّهَ كَانَ عَلَيْكُمْ رَقِيبًا ۝

O mankind be dutiful to your Lord, Who created you from a single person (Adam), and from him (Adam) He created his wife [Hawwa (Eve)], and from them both He created many men and women and fear Allāh (ﷻ) through Whom you demand your mutual (rights), and (do not cut the relations of) the wombs (kinship). Surely, Allāh (ﷻ) is Ever and All Watcher over you. (Qur'ān 4:1)

يَٰٓأَيُّهَا ٱلَّذِينَ ءَامَنُوا۟ ٱتَّقُوا۟ ٱللَّهَ وَقُولُوا۟ قَوْلًا سَدِيدًا ۝ يُصْلِحْ لَكُمْ أَعْمَٰلَكُمْ وَيَغْفِرْ لَكُمْ ذُنُوبَكُمْ ۗ وَمَن يُطِعِ ٱللَّهَ وَرَسُولَهُۥ فَقَدْ فَازَ فَوْزًا عَظِيمًا ۝

O you who believe! Keep your duty to Allāh (ﷻ) and fear Him, and speak (always) the truth. He will direct you to do righteous good deeds and will forgive you your sins. And whosoever obeys Allāh (ﷻ) and His Messenger (ﷺ) he has indeed achieved a great achievement (i.e. he will be saved from the Hell-fire and made to enter Paradise). (Qur'ān 33: 70,71)

Indeed, the most truthful speech is Allāh's Book, and the best guidance is that of Muḥammad (ﷺ). The most evil of affairs are newly invented ones (in the Religion), for every newly invented practice is an innovation (bid' ah), every innovation is misguidance, and every misguidance is in the Fire.

Allāh (ﷻ) has guided me to write this brief discourse on, *The Calamity of the Prophet's Death, and its Effects on the Muslim Nation.* I ask Allāh (ﷻ) by His grace and favour to make many people benefit from this work and to make that benefit great.

It is strange indeed that many students of knowledge and callers to Allāh (ﷻ) are unaware of the great calamity that is the Prophet's death, especially considering that he (ﷺ) himself pointed that out to us when he (ﷺ) said,

إِذَا أُصِيبَ أَحَدُكُم بِمُصِيبَةٍ، فَلْيَذْكُرْ مُصِيبَتَهُ بِي، فَإِنَّهَا أَعْظَمُ المَصَائِب.

8

"If one of you is afflicted with a calamity, then let him remember his calamity by me (i.e., by my death), for it is indeed the greatest of calamities."

The fact that we must be patient when disaster befalls us is not the only benefit we derive from this ḥadīth; rather, the ḥadīth is replete with many profound meanings, for it points out why man lives in darkness and at the same time shows him that safety and success lie in following the way of the Prophet (ﷺ).

The death of every great man has its effects on those who revere him. The effects of the Prophet's death are not limited to the Companions only, but extend to the entire Muslim Nation.

We must reflect on how the Prophet's death affected the individual and the Nation; perhaps, such a process of reflection might be the first step to changing our painful, present situation into one that is better and more dignified.

In this brief work, I have not dealt with all of the aspects of the Prophet's death – what occurred before and after, his sickness, or his last moments. I have instead chosen to limit the scope of this study to the effects of the Prophet's death on the Muslim Nation.

I ask Allāh (ﷻ) to accept this work of mine as well as the rest of my deeds; and I ask Him to benefit me and my brothers by this work.

The Death of the Messenger of Allāh (ﷺ) is the Greatest of Afflictions

Ibn 'Abbās (ﷺ) and Saabiṭ Al-Jumaḥee (ﷺ) both related that the Prophet (ﷺ) said,

إِذَا أُصِيبَ أَحَدُكُم بِمُصِيبَةٍ، فَلْيَذْكُر مُصِيبَتَهُ بِي، فَإِنَّهَا أَعْظَمُ المَصَائِب.

> "If one of you is afflicted with a calamity, then let him remember his calamity by me (i.e., by my death); for indeed, it is the greatest of calamities."[1]

It becomes clear to us from this ḥadīth that the death of the Prophet (ﷺ) is the greatest disaster that has occurred or will occur to the Muslim Nation. The Messenger of Allāh (ﷺ) requests that when we remember our calamities or afflictions, we should remember his death and his parting as well, a reflective process through which our other disasters will become insignificant in comparison.

Whenever we lost any of our relatives or loved-ones, we are sure to have felt the pain of parting and the anxiety of the farewell. The question now is this: Have we had any such feelings or sentiments when we contemplate the death of the Prophet (ﷺ).

What would happen if a man were to lose his entire family; his heart would ache and bleed while his tears would pour forth

---

[1] Related by Ibn Sa'd, al-Dārimī, and others; through other narrations that attest to it, it is authentic, as mentioned in *al-Ṣaḥīḥah* (106)

profusely. He marries after a period, and after many years pass, one of his sons dies. What is his sadness and pain if compared to the first calamity; is not the new affliction less painful in degree? And with that perspective – i.e., by remembering the death of the Prophet (ﷺ) – we should console ourselves whenever we are afflicted with a hardship.

The Messenger of Allāh (ﷺ) is addressing us, saying,

إنّ رسول الله (ﷺ) يخاطبنا فيقول: ((يا أيّها الناس! أيُّما أحدٍ من الناس – أو من المؤمنين – أُصيب بمصيبة؛ فليتعزَّ بمصيبته بي عن المصيبة التي تُصيبه بغيري؛ فإنّ أحداً من أُمّتي لن يُصاب بمصيبة بعدي أشدَّ عليه من مصيبتي.))

"O people, let any person – or any believer – who has been afflicted with a calamity remember his calamity by me and hence find solace in his calamity by any other person [or occurrence], for no one from my Nation will be afflicted by a calamity after me that is more severe upon him than my calamity."[2]

The Prophet's words, 'find solace' are indeed curative and healing words that are like medicine for the heart. What would happen if one were to lose his beloved parents in a car accident? Would not the effects of that calamity remain in his heart for the rest of his life? And what would happen if he lost his mother, wife, or son? Why is it that we feel nothing, yet we have been afflicted with the loss of the Prophet (ﷺ)? It is a calamity that outweighs all others when we contemplate the Prophet's statement:

---

[2] Related by Ibn Mājah, and narrated by ʿĀ'ishah (ﷺ) in *Ṣaḥīḥ Sunan Ibn Mājah* (No. 1300).

لا يؤمن أحدكم حتى أكون أحبّ إليه من ولدِه ووالده والناس
أجمعين.

"One of you does not believe until I am more beloved to him
than his child, his father, and all people."[3]

When we consider the ḥadīth before this one, it is as if this
ḥadīth means: Not one of you believes until my death becomes
a greater calamity for him than losing his son, his father, and all
people.

By Allāh, where are these feelings and sentiments? Yet they are
the feelings and sentiments of the true believer.

Have you lost your mother? And if so, when you were weeping
immediately after her death, did you remember that she took you
out of the darkness of her stomach to the light of the world, after
which she cared for you and raised you? Through the message of
the Messenger of Allāh (ﷺ), Allāh (ﷻ) has taken you out of the
darkness of misguidance and has brought you into the light of
guidance and *Tawḥīd* (Islamic Monotheism), and because of that
guidance – by the will of Allāh (ﷻ) – you are saved from eternity
in the Hellfire. But does the same hold true for your mother's
favours: are you saved from eternity in the Hellfire because of the
milk she fed you or because of her kindness and care?

By Allāh, in a single day, had I lost 1000 mothers, each equal
in kindness and love to my mother, it is not befitting for me to be
more sad on account of their loss than the sadness required from
me over the death of the Messenger of Allāh (ﷺ).

Have you lost your son? Do you not quickly burst into tears
when you remember his help, dutifulness, and love? No matter
what level these matters reach, they do not reach the level of what
the Prophet (ﷺ) conferred upon us. What he left for us will – by

---

[3] Bukhārī (15); Muslim (44)

12

the help of Allāh (ﷻ) – make us enter Paradise, whose width is equal to the heavens and the earth, a place of eternity and eternal bliss.

We are given pleasure by the help of our children and by their love, yet the years pass and fade away; however, the bliss of Paradise knows no end. Does not the Messenger of Allāh (ﷺ) deserve from us that we should be sadder over his death than over the death of anyone else; that we should remember him more than we remember anyone else we have lost, in terms of children, parents, and other loved ones?

The Prophet (ﷺ) Contributed and Left Behind More Good than did any Relative or Loved One

No matter how much love, care, or generosity we have received from a loved one or a relative, it does not even bear to be compared to the wonderful love, compassion, and care of the Prophet (ﷺ), for he (ﷺ) has shown us the way to achieving happiness and all that is good, while he has warned us away from all paths of evil and loss, whether it be regarding this world or the next. Who from our relatives, friends, or loved ones has made a similar contribution? Keep this in mind, and it will help you to truly feel the tragedy of losing the Prophet (ﷺ). To further appreciate the significance of the Prophet's guidance and lasting legacy, consider these questions:

- What if you entered the Hellfire?

- What if you were deprived of Paradise?

- What if you are punished in the grave?

- Who provides benefit to you? And what will save you from all of the above?

The Sentiments of the Companions (ﷺ) When the Prophet (ﷺ) Died

The reaction of the Companions regarding the Prophet's death is another affair altogether:

فعن سالم بن عُبيد (ﷺ)، قال: ((أغمي على رسول الله (ﷺ) في مرضه، فأفاق، فقال: حضرت الصلاة؟ فقالوا: نعم، فقال: مُروا بلالاً فليؤذِّن، ومُروا أبا بكر أن يصلِّي للنّاس – أو قال: بالنّاس –.

Sālim ibn 'Ubaid (ﷺ) related, During his sickness, the Prophet (ﷺ) became unconscious; when he later recovered consciousness, he said, 'Has the prayer arrived?' They said, 'Yes.' Then he said, 'Order Bilāl to perform the call to prayer, and order Abū Bakr to pray with the people (i.e., to lead the people in prayer).'

قال: ثم أُغمي عليه، فأفاق، فقال: حضرت الصلاة؟ فقالوا: نعم، فقال: مُروا بلالاً فليؤذِّن، ومُروا أبا بكر فليصلِّ بالنّاس، فقالت عائشة: إن أبي رجل أسيف؛ إذا قام ذلك المقام؛ بكى، فلا يستطيع، فلو أمرتَ غيره.

Then again, he lost consciousness; when he was revived, he said, 'Has the prayer arrived?' They said, 'Yes.' He (ﷺ) said, 'Order Bilāl to make the call to prayer, and order Abū Bakr to pray with the people.' 'Ā'ishah (ﷺ) said, 'My father is indeed a man who is quick to become sad and to cry; if he stands

15

in that position, he cries, and he is not able. Would that you
ordered someone else.'

قال: ثمّ أُغمي عليه فأفاق، فقال: مُروا بلالاً فليؤذّن، ومروا
أبا بكر فليصلّ بالنّاس؛ فإنّكنّ صواحبُ – أو صواحبات –
يوسُفَ.

He again lost consciousness, and when he revived this time,
he said, 'Order Bilāl to make the call to prayer, and order Abū
Bakr to pray with the people, for indeed, you women are the
companions of Yūsuf.'[4]

قال: فأُمر بلالٌ فأذّن، وأمر أبو بكر فصلّى بالنّاس.

ثمّ إنّ رسول الله (ﷺ) وجد خفّةً، فقال: انظروا لـي من أتّكىء
عليه، فجاءت بريرة ورجلٌ آخر، فاتّكأ عليهما، فلمّا رآه أبو
بكر؛ ذهب لِيَنْكُصَ، فأومأ إليه أن يثبت مكانه، حتى قضى أبو
بكر صلاته.

So Bilāl (ﷺ) was ordered to make the call to prayer and he
did so, and Abū Bakr (ﷺ) was ordered to lead the people in
prayer, and he did so. Then the Prophet (ﷺ) found some
energy, and he (ﷺ) said, 'Find someone for me upon whom
I may lean.' Barīrah and another man came, and he (ﷺ)
leaned upon them.[5] When Abū Bakr (ﷺ) saw him, he began
to move back so that the Prophet (ﷺ) could take his place,
but the Prophet (ﷺ) signalled to him that he should remain
firm in his place until Abū Bakr (ﷺ) completed his prayer.

---

[4] They are like the companions of Yūsuf in that they display outwardly
that which is opposite to what is in their inside. 'Ā'ishah (ﷺ) said her
statement so that people wouldn't be pessimistic about her father, an
explanation that is related in Bukhārī and Muslim.

[5] Our Shaykh – may Allāh have mercy on him – said, 'He went out, leaning
on 'Abbās (ﷺ) and another man, who was 'Alī ibn Abī Ṭālib (ﷺ). It is said
that the two men were 'Abbās (ﷺ) and his son, Faḍl (ﷺ). It is understood
from the different narrations that the Prophet (ﷺ) went out on numerous
occasions in this manner.

ثمَّ إنَّ رسول الله (ﷺ) قُبض، فقال عـمر: والله لا أسمع أحداً
يذكر أنَّ رسول الله (ﷺ) قبض؛ إلا ضربتُه بسيفي هذا)).

Then the Messenger of Allāh (ﷺ) died, yet ʿUmar (ﷺ) said,
'By Allāh, if anyone mentions that the Messenger of Allāh (ﷺ)
has died, I will strike him with this sword of mine.'

قال: وكان الناس أُمّيّين، لم يكن فيهم نبيٌ قبله، فأمسك الناس،
فقالوا: يا سالمُ! انطلق إلى صاحب رسول الله (ﷺ)، فادْعهُ،
فأتيتُ أبا بكر وهو في المسجد، فأتيته أبكي دهشاً، فلمّا رآني؛
قال لي: أقُبِض رسول الله (ﷺ)؟

قلتُ: إن عمر يقول: لا أسمعُ أحداً يذكرُ أن رسول الله (ﷺ)
قبض؛ إلا ضربتُه بسيفي هذا!

The people were illiterate: never before Muḥammad (ﷺ)
was there a Prophet among them. The people desisted [from
any action] and said, 'O Sālim, go to the Messenger of Allāh's
companion and call him.' So I went to Abū Bakr (ﷺ) while
he was in the Mosque. As I approached him, I was crying in
bewilderment. When he saw me, he said, 'Did the Messenger
of Allāh (ﷺ) die?' I said, 'Indeed, ʿUmar (ﷺ) says: If I hear
anyone mention that the Messenger of Allāh (ﷺ) died, I will
strike him with this sword of mine.'

فقال لي: انطلق. فانطلقتُ معه، فجاء والناس قد دخلوا على
رسول الله (ﷺ)، فقال: يا أيها الناس! أفرجوا لي، فأفرجوا له،
فجاء حتى أكبّ عليه ومسّه، فقال: ﴿إِنَّكَ مَيِّتٌ وَإِنَّهُم مَّيِّتُونَ﴾

Abū Bakr (ﷺ) then said to me, 'Proceed,' and so I proceeded
with him until he reached the people, who had entered upon
the Messenger of Allāh (ﷺ). He (ﷺ) said, 'O people! Make
way for me.' They made way for him until he bent down to
the Prophet (ﷺ) and touched him; he then said:

Verily, you (O Muḥammad (ﷺ) will die and verily, they (too) will die. (Qur'ān 39:30)

ثمَّ قالوا: يا صاحب رسول الله (ﷺ)! أَقُبِضَ رسول الله (ﷺ)؟ قال: نعم، فعَلِموا أن قد صدق.

The people said, 'O companion of the Messenger of Allāh (ﷺ), has the Messenger of Allāh (ﷺ) died?' He answered, 'Yes.' And they knew that he had spoken the truth.

قالوا: يا صاحب رسول الله (ﷺ)! أيُصلّى على رسول الله (ﷺ)؟

قال: نعم، قالوا: وكيف؟ قال: يدخُلُ قومٌ، فيكبِّرون ويصلُّون ويدعون: ثمَّ يخرجون، ثمَّ يدخل قومٌ، فيكبِّرون ويصلُّون و يدعون، ثمَّ يخرجون ...

They said, 'O companion of the Messenger of Allāh! Is the Messenger of Allāh (ﷺ) to be prayed upon?' He (ﷺ) said, 'Yes.' 'And how?' They asked. He replied, 'A group enters to magnify Allāh, pray to Him, and invoke him. Then they leave, after which another group enters, who magnify Allāh, pray to Him, and invoke Him, after which they leave...'

قالوا: يا صاحب رسول الله (ﷺ)! أيُدفَنُ رسول الله (ﷺ)؟

قال: نعم، قالوا: أين؟ قال: في المكان الذي قَبض الله فيه روحه؛ فإنَّ الله لم يقبضْ روحه إلا في مكان طيّب. فعلِموا أنْ قد صدَق.

ثمَّ أمرهُم أن يغسِّلَه بنو أبيه ...

The people asked, 'O companion of the Messenger of Allāh! Is the Messenger of Allāh (ﷺ) to be buried?' He said, 'Yes.' They said, 'Where?' He answered, 'In the same place that Allāh took his soul, for indeed, Allāh did not take his soul except in a good and pure place.' And they knew that he had spoken the truth. Then he ordered the offspring from the Prophet's father's side to wash him[6]...[7]

'Umar (ﷺ) said, "By Allāh, if I hear anyone mention that the Messenger of Allāh (ﷺ) has died, I will strike him with this sword of mine!"

Why would 'Umar (ﷺ) threaten others with his sword, if not because of his great love of the Messenger of Allāh (ﷺ). He loved the Messenger of Allāh (ﷺ) more than he loved his own self, his son, his wife, his wealth, and all of mankind. His reaction when he heard someone say, "The Messenger of Allāh (ﷺ) has died," is completely understandable.

As for the rest of the Companions, they refrained from speaking. Because there never was a Prophet among them before the Messenger of Allāh (ﷺ), they knew not what to do. But Abū Bakr (ﷺ), who went to the Prophet (ﷺ) and touched him, recited:

إِنَّكَ مَيِّتٌ وَإِنَّهُم مَّيِّتُونَ

Verily, you (O Muḥammad (ﷺ) will die and verily, they (too) will die. (Qur'ān 39:30)

His recitation here points to his profound understanding of the Noble Qur'ān; he understood from this verse that death is inevitable – even for the Prophet (ﷺ). The rest of the companions

---

[6] In *Al-Shamāil*, Our Shaykh – may Allāh have mercy on him – said, 'i.e., his male inheriting relatives. And so 'Ali (ﷺ) washed him. Al-Faḍl ibn 'Abbās (ﷺ), Usāmah (ﷺ), and Shaqrān (the freed slave of the Messenger of Allāh (ﷺ)) would pass the water on to 'Ali (ﷺ).'

[7] The entire narration is related by Al-Tirmidhī in *Al-Shamāil*; by Ibn Mājah in *Al-Ṣalāh* (The chapter on the Messenger of Allāh's prayer during his sickness); by Al-Ṭabarānī, in *Al-Kabīr*; part of it by al-Bukhārī, in his *Ṣaḥīḥ*; and part of it by Al-Nisā'ī. It is also related in *Mukhtaṣir Al-Shamā'il* (333).

were so shocked that they passed through a phase of denial, and no wonder, for the one they lost was the Messenger of Allāh (ﷺ).

How many times have we heard of people who fell unconscious upon hearing the news of their child's death; for some, the shock led to a stroke, causing them to die instantly; others lost their mind or suffered from some dangerous sickness.

"The people said, 'O companion of the Messenger of Allāh (ﷺ), has the Messenger of Allāh (ﷺ) died?' He answered, 'Yes.' And they knew that he had spoken the truth." It was at this point that the Companions calmed down, knowing that the Messenger of Allāh (ﷺ) had indeed died.

وعن أنس (ﷺ)، قال: لـمّا كان اليوم الذي دخل فيه رسول الله (ﷺ) المدينة؛ أضاء منها كلُّ شيء، فلـمّا كان اليوم الذي مات فيه؛ أظلم منها كل شيءٍ، وما نفَضْنا عن النّبيّ (ﷺ) الأيدي حتى أنكرْنا قلوبنا.

Anas (ﷺ) related,

On the day that the Messenger of Allāh (ﷺ) entered Madīnah, all things inside of it became illuminated. But on the day that he died, all things in it became darkened. And no sooner did we leave the Prophet (ﷺ) and bury him than we reproached our hearts (i.e., they did not find their hearts to be upon the same degree of purity as before the Prophet's death, when revelation was still being revealed to him, and when he was still teaching them).[8]

"On the day that the Messenger of Allāh (ﷺ) entered Madīnah, all things inside of it became illuminated": Everything was gleaming because of the Messenger of Allāh's presence and arrival; happiness filled the hearts of the young and old, males and females. But on the day he (ﷺ) died, all things became darkened. The landscape and scenery around them changed: they found

---

[8] Ibn Mājah, in *Ṣaḥīḥ Ibn Mājah* (1322).

no taste in the delicious, no beauty in the beautiful. Their souls became constricted.

As soon as they parted from the Prophet (ﷺ) and finished burying him, they reproached their hearts, which became different from the hearts that they had known during his lifetime. So piercing and delicate were their emotions and feelings, they sensed a slight change that to others would probably have remained imperceptible.

The Crying of Umm Aiyman (ﷺ), and how She Moved Abū Bakr (ﷺ) and ʿUmar (ﷺ) to Tears

((عن أنس (ﷺ) قال: ((قال أبو بكر – (ﷺ) – بعد وفاة رسول الله (ﷺ) – لعمر: انطلقْ بنا إلــــى أُمِّ أيمن نزورها كما كان رسول الله (ﷺ) يزورها، فلما انتهينا إليها بكتْ، فقالا لها: ما يبكيكِ؟ ما عند الله خيرٌ لرسول الله (ﷺ)؟ فقالت: ما أبكي أن لا أكون أَعْلَم أنَّ ما عند الله خيرٌ لرسول الله (ﷺ)، ولكن أبكي أنَّ الوحي قد انقطع من السماء، فهيّجتهما على البكاء، فجعلا يبكيان معها))

Anas (ﷺ) said,

> After the Messenger of Allāh (ﷺ) died, Abū Bakr (ﷺ) said to ʿUmar (ﷺ), "Come with us to Umm Aiyman[9]; we shall visit her as the Messenger of Allāh (ﷺ) used to visit her." When we reached her, she was crying, so they (Abū Bakr (ﷺ) and ʿUmar (ﷺ)) said, "What makes you cry? Is not what Allāh has with Him better for the Messenger of Allāh (ﷺ)?" She said, "I do not cry being ignorant of the fact that that which is with Allāh is better for the Messenger of Allāh (ﷺ); rather, I cry because revelation has ceased to come down from the sky." She moved the two of them so much [with her words] that they began to cry with her.[10]

---

[9] She was the Prophet's nurse, and during his childhood, his servant.

[10] Muslim (2454)

The Messenger of Allāh (ﷺ) was Peace (*Amanah*) for his Companions (ﷺ)

عن أبي موسى (ﷺ) ، عن النّبيّ (ﷺ)، قال: ((النّجومُ أَمَنَةٌ للسماء، فإذا ذهبت النجومُ؛ أتى السماء ما توعدُ، وأنا أَمنةٌ لأصحابي، فإذا ذهبْتُ؛ أتى أصحابي ما يوعدون، وأصحابي أمنةٌ لأمّتي، فإذا ذهب أصحابي؛ أتى أمّتي ما يوعدون)).

Abū Mūsa (ﷺ) related that the Prophet (ﷺ) said,

> The stars are peace (*amanah*)[11] to the sky: when the stars leave (i.e., when the are scattered), what has been promised to the sky will come to it (i.e., it will split apart). I am peace (*amanah*) to my Companions: when I leave, what has been promised to my Companions will come to them (i.e., trials, wars, and discord). And my Companions are peace (*amanah*) for my Nation: when my Companions leave, what has been promised to my Nation will come to it (i.e., the appearance of innovations, the overcoming of desires, etc.).

What will happen when the stars are gone? The features of life will change: there will occur cataclysmic, violent, and awesome changes. In a different sense, the same can be said about the parting of the Prophet (ﷺ) from the Companions (ﷺ): their life and affairs changed; strife and discord occurred among them.

---

[11] Peace, meaning that the stars are the reason for peace in the sky; as long as the stars remain, the sky will not split apart or break, nor will its inhabitants die.

And with the parting of the Companions (ﷺ) there occurred much strife in our Nation, which suddenly became afflicted with many trials and calamities. Innovation became Sunnah in the minds of people and vice versa; people began to see good as evil and evil as good. Ignorance spread and knowledge almost became extinct had it not been for the small number of Allāh's slaves, whom Allāh (ﷻ) favoured with his mercy.

People ceased to rule by what Allāh (ﷻ) revealed, and Islāmic rulings were used to promote desires, ambitions, and lusts. Muslims became divided into many groups.

And this reminds us of what is authentically related from Ibn Mas'ūd (ﷺ) – a narration that can correctly be ascribed to the Prophet (ﷺ):

((كيف أنتم إذا لَبِستكُم فتنةٌ؛ يَهْرَم فيها الكبير، ويربو فيها الصغير، ويتّخذُها الناس سُنّةً، إذا تُرك منها شيء قيل: تُركت السُّنّةُ؟، قالوا: ومتى ذاك؟ قال: ((إذا ذهبت عُلماؤُكم، وكثُرت قُرّاؤكم، وقَلَّت فقهاؤُكم، وكثرت أُمراؤكم، وقلَّت أُمناؤكم، والتُمِسَتِ الدُّنيا بعمل الآخرة، وتُفُقِّه لغير الدين))).

"How will you be when you will be enveloped by a trial, [through which] the old will reach senility and the young will grow. People will take it to be a Sunnah, and if any part of it is left, it will be said, 'has a Sunnah been left?" They asked, "And when is that?" He said, "When your scholars are gone; when your reciters will increase in number; when your *Fuqahā* will be few in number; when the number of rulers increases;when the trustwrothy ones will be few; when the world is sought through the actions of the Hereafter; and when knowledge of the Religion is sought, but not for the Religion."[12]

---

[12] Related by al-Dārimī (1/64), with two chains, one of which is authentic, and the other of which is *hasan* (acceptable); by Ḥakim (4/514), and by

→

If what was promised to our Nation arrived as soon as the Companions were gone, then imagine the effect of the Prophet's death!

---

others, as has been related by our Shaykh, Al-Albānī (may Allāh have mercy on him) in *Qiyām Ramaḍān*.

Refuting those who Say that the Death of the Prophet (ﷺ) Was not a Calamity

Those who make this claim say, "This is Allāh's Noble Book and this is the pure Sunnah of the Messenger of Allāh (ﷺ), so what is there to fear regarding the death of the Messenger of Allāh (ﷺ)?"

The Prophet (ﷺ) answered them in the following ḥadīth.

عن زيد بن لبيد (﵁) قال: ((ذكر النّبيّ (ﷺ) شيئاً، فقال: ذاك عند أوان ذهاب العلم.

قلت: يا رسول الله! وكيف يذهب العلم ونحنُ نقرأُ القرآن، ونُقرِئُهُ أبناءنا، ويُقرِئُهُ أبناؤنا أبناءهم إلى يوم القيامة؟!

قال: ثكلتك أُمُّك زيادُ! إنْ كُنتُ لأراك من أفقه رجلٍ بالمدينة، أَوَليس هـذه اليهـود والنّصارى يقرؤون التوراة والإنجيل؟ لا يعملون بشيءٍ مما فيهما!))

Zayd ibn Lubayd (﵁) related,

> The Prophet (ﷺ) mentioned something and then said, "That is when knowledge departs." I said, 'O Messenger of Allāh! How will knowledge depart when we recite the Qur'ān, teach its recitation to our children – with each generation teaching their children until the Day of Resurrection?'

He (ﷺ) said, "Ziyād, may your mother lose you! I had seen you as the one most possessed of understanding in Madinah. Do not the Jews and Christians recite the Torah and the Bible? Yet they apply nothing that is in them!"[13]

Before us we have Allāh's Book and the Prophet's Sunnah, but where is the practical application of the two? And who conveys their messages to others? But before action and propagation, where is the authentic knowledge? Therefore, there is no place for a claim such as the one being discussed here, nor is it anywhere near the truth.

The entire Muslim Nation was pleased with Muḥammad (ﷺ) as their Messenger, Prophet, leader, ruler, and educator. Whom does the Muslim Nation agree upon today? Would that we truly understood how the world was during his time and how it has become now. Muslims enjoyed honour, superiority, and status, and here we find ourselves now – in the depths of darkness, hoping for mercy from the 'greater' nations of today, fearing lest they destroy and subjugate us.

In the newspapers, we read about what we are afflicted with – death, subjugation, tyranny, and plots that are weaved in order to destroy us. Among our own ranks, we are afflicted by partisanship and division, each group being satisfied and pleased with what it has. In the name of Islām – Islām, scholars, and callers to Islām are attacked; and in the name of the Prophet's family, people curse the Prophet's family. Few are the seekers of Paradise, many the seekers of the Hellfire.

People have fabricated lies upon the Messenger of Allāh (ﷺ), and it has become difficult for the masses to distinguish between the authentic and the weak; it has become easy for every man

---

[13] Related by Al-Tirmidhī, Aḥmad, Ibn Mājah in *Ṣaḥiḥ Ibn Mājah* (3272), and others.

27

of desire to fabricate *aḥādīth*. Innovations are revered as if they represent the foundations and pillars of Islām. The man of the Sunnah is considered to be an innovator, and the innovator is considered to be a man of the Sunnah!

There is a vast wilderness that separates us from the truth. If one gives a speech, saying, "The Messenger of Allāh (ﷺ) said," we would have to search out for its authenticity, not knowing, will we meet one whom Allāh (ﷺ) has blessed with the true and precise criteria with which he is able to distinguish the authentic from the weak.

And if the ḥadīth that is quoted ends up being authentic – unfortunately, it is very often weak – we must acquaint ourselves with the true meanings of the ḥadīth and the rulings that it imparts. We must plunge into the depths of the principles of *Fiqh*, perhaps that we may come onto the shores of safety with results – with a further necessity of plunging into the depths of the Arabic language, its rules, idioms, and nuances.

After all of that, even if we finally arrive at safety, we forget to apply that which we have learnt, and we sit idle, not conveying to others the message – except for those whom Allāh has shown mercy to, and few they are indeed.

Are not all of the above-mentioned calamities and difficulties from the results of the Prophet's death? Are they not also from the results of the death of his Companions (ﷺ)? Are they not also from the results of not applying Allāh's Book and His Messenger's Sunnah?

After the Death of the Prophet (ﷺ)

Eyes have shed their tears and hearts have quaked, but what does one do? The answer is to apply Allāh's Book and the Messenger of Allāh's Sunnah, for the Messenger of Allāh (ﷺ) has informed us that the Jews and Christians strayed because they did not apply the Torah and the Bible.

Therefore we must work, scrutinising texts, taking those narrations that are acceptable, and leaving those that are not. This affair is Religion and Law, so let us see whom it is we take our Religion from.[14] We must learn, but more to the point, learn from scholars.

Let us contemplate the advice of 'Umar ibn 'Abdul-'Azīz (May Allāh have mercy on him), as he was writing to Abū Bakr ibn Ḥazm,

((انظر ما كان من حديث رسول الله (ﷺ) فاكتبه؛ وإنِّي خِفْتُ دروس العلم، وَذَهَاب العلماء؛ ولا تقبل إلا حديث النّبيّ (ﷺ).

ولْتُفشوا العلم، ولْتَجْلِسوا حتى يُعلَّم من لا يعْلَم؛ فإنّ العلم لا يهلِكُ حتى يكون سِرًّا)).

"Gather the ḥadīth of the Messenger of Allāh (ﷺ) and write it down, for I fear the disappearance of knowledge and the passing away of scholars. And accept only the ḥadīth of the Prophet (ﷺ). Spread knowledge and sit to teach until he

---

[14] This is a saying of Muḥammad ibn Sīrīn – may Allāh have mercy on him.

is taught who does not know, for indeed, knowledge is not destroyed until it becomes a secret."[15]

In a sense, through gatherings of knowledge, we accompany the Prophet (ﷺ). An Arab poet said,

> The people of ḥadīth are the people of the Messenger of Allāh (ﷺ)
>
> If they do not accompany him in person, they accompany his breaths and utterances.

So let us accompany the Messenger of Allāh (ﷺ) in his prayer, in his fast, in his *Zakāt*, in his *Ḥajj*, in his behaviour, and in his *Jihād*. And let us accept only the ḥadīth of the Prophet (ﷺ).[16] His ḥadīth is a cure and a light; in it there is safety, success, and happiness.

---

[15] Al-Bukhārī: The Book of Knowledge; Chapter: How Knowledge is Removed, *muʿallaq*, but with words that evince sureness. Al-Ḥāfiẓ related that Abū Nuʿaym included it connected in *Akhbār Aṣbahān*.

[16] This does not suggest that one should not benefit from the sayings and interpretations and rulings of the scholars, for indeed, misguidance lies in forsaking their books and understanding, just as misguidance lies in blindly and intransigently following their sayings, or giving preference to them over the ḥadīth of the Prophet (ﷺ).

Contemplate his Final Advice

All excellent people with their passing leave behind important advice; has the Messenger of Allāh (ﷺ) left for us some final advice? Yes, he has left for us words that constitute a most comprehensive set of advices and admonitions.

عن عبدالرحمن بن عمرو السلمي، عن العرباض بن سارية (رضي الله عنه) وكان من البكّائين-، قال: ((صلّى رسول الله (ﷺ) الغداة، ثمّ أقبل علينا بوجهه، فوعظَنا موعظةً بليغةً، ذرفت منها الأعين، ووجلت منها القلوب، فقال رجل: يا رسول الله! كأنّ هذه موعظةُ مودّع؟! فقال اتقوا الله، وعليكم بالسمع والطاعة، وإنْ عبداً حبشياً، وإنّه من يعِش منكم بعدي؛ فسيرى اختلافاً كثيراً؛ فعليكم بسنتي وسنّة الخلفاء من بعدي الراشدين المهديين، عضُّوا عليها بالنّواجذ وإيّاكم ومحدثات الأُمور؛ فإنّ كلَّ بدعةٍ ضلالة)).

'Abdur-Rahmān ibn 'Amr Al-Salamī related that 'Irbād ibn Sāriyah (ﷺ) – who was known for his gentle nature and frequent crying – said,

> The Messenger of Allāh (ﷺ) prayed in the early morning and then faced us. He delivered to us an eloquent and profound sermon, one that caused eyes to shed tears and hearts to quake. A man said, 'O Messenger of Allāh! It is as if this is a farewell sermon!' He (ﷺ) said, 'Fear Allāh, and upon you is to listen and obey (i.e. to those in authority), even if he (i.e., the one in authority) is an Ethiopian slave. Whoever from you lives after me will see much conflict; then upon you is my Sunnah and the Sunnah of the rightly-guided Khalīfahs

31

after me: bite on it (i.e. my Sunnah...) with your molars. And beware and stay away from innovated matters, for every innovation is misguidance.[17]

We must contemplate this sermon; we must live with it and have it live with us; and we must remember it in all of the affairs of our lives – in times of ease, pain, happiness, and tragedy; in times of peace and trial; in times of harmony and discord, for indeed, it is a sermon that contains in it the ingredients of happiness, the secrets of safety and success.

---

[17] Related by Abū Dāwūd in *Ṣaḥīḥ Abī Dāwūd* (3851), by Al-Tirmidhī in *Ṣaḥīḥ Sunan Al-Tirmidhī* (2157), and by Ibn Mājah in *Ṣaḥīḥ Sunan Ibn Mājah* (40)